SISYPHA LARVATA PRODEAT

(SISYPHA WEARING A MASK ADVANCES)

薛西法假面潛行

SISYPHA LARVATA PRODEAT
(SISYPHA WEARING A MASK ADVANCES)

薛西法假面潛行

poems by
Jan Cole

珍·柯爾詩集

MADVILLE
PUBLISHING

Lake Dallas, Texas

SECOND EDITION
Requests for permission to reproduce material from this work
should be sent to:

Permissions
Madville Publishing LLC
P.O. Box 358
Lake Dallas, TX 75065

Poet: Jan Cole   詩人：珍·柯爾
Artist: Adelina Moya   畫家：雅德琳娜·摩亞
Translator: Angela Liu   翻譯：楊愛蘭
Editor: Lorrie Lo Wagamon   編譯：駱珞
Design: Kim Davis   設計：金·戴維斯

ISBN: 978-1-948692-00-7
Library of Congress Control Number: 2018948230

The production of this book was made possible in part by a grant
from the Huntsville Arts Commission.

Table of Contents 目錄

About the Author   作者簡介   ix

La Vie   生活

Sisypha Quest	薛西法之問	1
Fame Conceit Humility	聲名 自負 謙虛	2
Haiku	俳句	3
The Performing Dog	雜耍狗	5
Reality	真象	6
H.......	H⋯⋯	7
The Frog	青蛙	8
Culture Shock	文化衝擊	9
Vulnerability	脆弱	11
"Carpe Diem!"	"把握今朝！"	12
Limerick for "La Vie"	"生活"五行詩	13

Forward Movement   前進運動

The Tightrope Walker	走鋼絲者	17
La Branche (the Branch)	樹枝	19
Ambition	抱負	20
To the Gregarious Artists...	致喜好群聚的藝術家⋯	21
Southern Hommage	南腔致敬	22
Herz Und Die Zauberflöte	心與魔笛	25
Limerick of Forward Movement	前進運動五行詩	27

Masks   面具

The Mask Collection	面具收藏	31
The Misanthrope	厭世者	32
Mardi Gras	嘉年華	34
Depression	憂鬱	35
Communication	溝通	35
Sisypha Larvata Prodeat	薛西法假面潛行	37

Limerick of Outward   對外看齊 (面具)   40
   Conformity (Masks)   五行詩

Politics And Arson   政治與縱火

A Visit to H.......   訪H⋯⋯   43
Poem for a Rock Song   一首搖滾詩   44
Poem in Angry Desolation   一首悲憤詩   46
A Conversation Overheard   夢中偶聞   48
   in a Dream
Limerick of Arson   縱火五行詩   52

De L'amour Non Partagé   不能分享的愛

The Amature Horticulturist   業餘園藝家   54
For My German Apollo   給我的德國阿波羅   56
Fishin' Trip   釣魚行   58
A Titillation   動情   60
A Cynical View   嘲諷之見   62
Smotherly Love   窒息的愛   63
Hypersensitivity   超級敏感   64
To My Pink Rabbit   給我的粉紅兔   66
"Dream"   "夢"   68
Orpheus   奧菲斯   70
Love and Pig Limerick   愛情與豬五行詩   72

Friends   友儕

A Jazz Sonnet In 5/4   5/4拍爵士樂十四行詩   74
Duo for Mezzo and Flute   女中音與長笛協奏   76
Pour Robert Veyron-Lacroix   致羅伯·威宏–拉克羅   76
Poem for a Brilliant Friend   詩致一絕妙好友   78
La Connaissance Des Gens   人的認知及其他   79
   et la Suite
Eyes—A Tribute to Daddy   眼睛—獻給父親   80
Two Don Quijotes   兩位唐吉軻德   82
A Note is Played   一聲音符奏出   83

Sonnet in "Shanghai East"	"浦東"裏的十四行詩	84
Pour Jean-Pierre Rampal	致尚–皮耶·郎帕爾	86
"Akasha"	"阿卡夏"	88
A Dactylic Meandering	婉約長短調	90
A Paean	一首歡樂歌	92
for Alois Hessling	給阿洛意司·黑思靈	
Sonnet	十四行詩	94
The Eaglet	雛鷹	96
Chevalier De Medici	麥地奇家的騎士	97
The Feather Crutch	羽毛拐杖	98
Different Emphasis	重點不同	100
Limerick of Friendship	友情五行詩	101
Afterword	**後語**	103
Biographies	**簡介**	109
Acknowledgments	**致謝**	112

About the Author

Jan Carroll Cole
August 26, 1940—July 07, 2019

This collection of poems was first published in 1987 when poet Jan Cole lived and worked in San Francisco, but the poems were written over the course of many years, beginning with her time in university at the Newcomb College of Tulane University and at the Sorbonne. Many of the poems are set in the town of Huntsville, Texas, where Jan was raised and lived until July of 2019. Other poems in the collection reference friends Jan knew and worked with around the world.

Among her numerous musical accolades, Jan recalls the following especially: She wrote a musical score for Robert Yee's film for the San Diego Underwater Film Festival. She was named Composer of the Year by the Bay Area Critics Association for a musical for *Theatre Rhinoceros* in San Francisco. She was the Music Director for the Missouri Repertory Theatre's production of the musical based on Tolstoy's *Strider the Horse*. Artist in Residence, Ying Ruo-Cheung invited her to write a new music score to his translation of the ancient Peking opera, *Fifteen Strings of Cash*, using Chinese and American percussion instruments.

Jan had a 3000-year-old Egyptian arched harp reconstructed and played it at the opening of the King Tut Exhibit in New Orleans. She recently had a replica of King David's lyre built in Jerusalem, on which she composed a song to Psalm 23 for her friend Kathryn McKenzie.

Jan played guitar, mandolin, banjo, recorders, banjo-lute, ukulele, dulcimer, and flutes. She studied flute with Jean-Pierre Rampal, and one of her top students, Patty Mills, won a Fulbright Scholarship to study with Monsieur Rampal at the Paris Conservatoire.

作者簡介

珍·柯爾女士這本詩集曾於1987年在三藩市首次出版。它的創作時期涵蓋多年，最早可溯至她在新奧爾良杜蘭大學紐康學院就讀，以及她留學巴黎大學時期。其中有好幾首詩寫到了德州的亨次維爾，她的成長之地以及目前居住的地方。其他也有幾首涉及她在世界各地結識並共事過的朋友。

她的一生成就非凡，在所獲的無數榮耀當中她特別難忘：她曾為羅伯·易先生入選聖地牙哥水下影片展的作品作曲；她曾被三番市灣區犀牛劇場樂評人協會評為"年度作曲家"；她曾任密蘇里大學劇場製作的托爾斯泰「馬兒史踹得」改編音樂劇的音樂總監；那時遇到了駐校藝術家英若誠先生，也曾受邀為他英譯的古老中國崑曲「十五貫」，用中，美打擊樂器譜曲。

珍有一把改造過的，有三千年歷史的埃及弓型豎琴。她曾用它演奏，為紐奧良的圖坦卡門法老寶藏展覽開幕式助興。最近她應朋友凱薩琳·麥肯齊女士之請，也曾用耶路撒冷複製的一把大衛王里拉琴，為聖詩詩篇第23首譜了一曲。

此外，珍也會彈吉他，曼陀林，斑鳩琴，直琴，琵琶，優客麗麗，揚琴和長笛。她師從長笛大師尚–皮耶·郎帕爾先生。她教導的優秀學生之一，派蒂·蜜兒女士，也獲得了傅爾布萊特獎學金，到巴黎音樂學院，隨郎帕爾大師學習。

SISYPHA LARVATA PRODEAT
(Sisypha Wearing a Mask Advances)

薛西法假面潛行

La Vie
生活

SISYPHA QUEST

If I push this rock
to the top of the hill
and then stop,
it will roll down
the other side.

But I was wondering
if I could push just hard enough
for the rock to stay
in the same place,
like a car on an incline
when you let the
clutch out
so it moves neither forward
nor backward.

The car gave the answer:
The clutch wears out.

薛西法之問

我若將這塊巨石
推至山頂
然後停住，
它會從另一邊
滾下去。

但我也曾想
如果我推的力道夠巧
或許能讓巨石
定點停住，
就像上坡的車
鬆開
離合器
它能不進
也不退。

車子的回答是:
離合器用多了會壞。

FAME
CONCEIT
HUMILITY

聲名
自負
謙虛

A balloon ride in the air
And never knowing where
It will land

乘著氣球隨風吹
從不知它會
落腳何地

A pin into the ball
A heavy painful fall
No helping hand

若一針將球刺穿
會跌得很慘
無人救急

A ride unto the end
It gently will descend
Onto the sand

倘有幸飄至終站
則可能緩緩
降抵沙地

HAIKU

俳句

Don't go with current
It leads to the waterfall
You're not a salmon

勿隨波逐流
它會帶你至瀑布
而你非鮭魚

THE PERFORMING DOG 雜耍狗

A performing dog
Taught
Then pushed by will power
To perform life's routine
Correctly—
     To do cute tricks upon demand
     To lick always the feeding hand
     To bark in joy at clever remarks
Sometimes rebels.
The sugarcoated mask dissolves,
Letting her see
And clash with herself
And want to be free.

一隻雜耍狗
經過訓練
再加以意志操控
便可以機械般無誤地
表演—
     聽指令耍寶
     舔餵食者手
     應讚聲歡叫
但有時也難免反抗。
糖衣面具總會溶化，
牠會因此看清真相
而心生衝突
而嚮往自由。

REALITY

真象

How does one best see
A star?
By looking at it
Indirectly.
But you cannot always
See it . . .
It depends on
Weather conditions
And
Reflections.

如何觀星
最棒?
間接的
注視它。
不過也不是想看就能
看到…
還有賴當時的
天候
與
反光。

H.......

Sitting ducks in a pond
Death is the hunter
No moving water
To disturb his aim
Just wait for Death
And he will come
Wait in stillness.

H........

停在池中的鴨子
死神是牠的獵者
沒有晃動的水波
干擾準頭
就等死神了
靜待中
祂一定到。

THE FROG

青蛙

A frog
Swimming beneath the surface of a pond
Needed air
And wanted to see her reflection
So she perched upon a lily pad.
For a moment her image was clear,
But from the sinking pad came ripples
And the vision was blurred.
She forgot her wish
And plunged into the cool depths . . .
Only to have to recommence
Her painful ascent.

一隻青蛙
游在池水下
需要呼吸
也想看看自己的倒影
因此牠跳上了一片蓮葉。
有一瞬間牠看清了自己，
可是蓮葉下沉掀起漣漪
又糢糊了那影。
牠忘了初衷
一頭又跳入深冷水中…
只好再次
辛苦的往上游。

CULTURE SHOCK

for Janet Adderley

All right
Yes
Just a little light
Let it in
But not too much at once
It's blinding
(I've misplaced my sunglasses)
All that beauty,
That perfection—
Just a little bit
At a time.

文化衝擊

寫給珍娜·阿得蕾

好的
可以
讓一點光
進來
但不要一下子太多
會閃瞎我
(我的墨鏡不見了)
所有的那些亮麗，
那些完美-
一次只要
一點點。

VULNERABILITY
The Shark

If the shark smells blood
He will kill you and eat you
If he can
Even if he liked you
Before you were bleeding
(He can't help his natural instinct)
But if you want to live
When you are wounded,
Don't let the shark know.

脆弱
鯊魚

一隻鯊魚聞到血腥
會想盡辦法
將你吞噬
即便在你流血之前
他對你還滿有意思
(天性如此沒有辦法)
所以如果你受了傷
卻還想活命的話,
千萬別讓鯊魚知悉。

"CARPE DIEM!"

"把握今朝!"

"Carpe diem," they used to say
But I ease gently into the day
"Hitch your wagon to a star!"
But with no air, could one fly far?

Ambition is a lofty call
    But I must be realistic—
To butt my head against a wall
    May seem a bit simplistic

I may go straight from "here" to "there"
    But often times hit muck . . .
My goal is clear but how I fare
    Depends on drive and luck.

"把握今朝,"人們總這麼說
我卻日子悠閒過
"乘著馬車到天邊!"
沒有風,何能行遠?

抱負是個崇高的理想
    我卻必須講求實在-
一味以頭撞牆
    只會顯得有點呆

由"此處"到"彼處"我可直通
    只不過常踩到狗屎…
我的目標明確但是否成功
    還有賴動力與運時。

LIMERICK FOR "LA VIE" "生活"五行詩

A salmon, balloon and a shark 鮭魚，氣球，鯊
A frog, a sports car and a bark 青蛙，跑車，狗叫大
    Tho' life can be witty, 　　　雖說人生可以機智，
    Sometimes it's a pity 　　　可惜仍無法忽視
That before seeing light, there's much dark. 光明之前，一片黑壓壓。

Forward Movement

前進運動

THE TIGHTROPE WALKER 走鋼絲者

Giddy tightrope walker   令人目眩的走鋼絲者
Skillfully wobbling along the wire   熟練的沿繩搖晃前進
Destination single, certain   目標單一，明確
Arrival inevitable   一定到得了
If she can   只要她能
But keep   一直保持
Her balance   平衡

LA BRANCHE

Une branche
Qui flottait dans un fleuve
Voulait échapper de l'eau courante
Pour la regarder
Mais quand elle est montée
Sur la rive
Le soleil l'a séchée.

THE BRANCH

A branch
That was floating in a river
Wanted to escape the rushing water
In order to look at it
But when she climbed up
on the bank
The sun dried her up.

樹枝

漂在河中的
一根樹枝
很想逃出急流
與河對視
上得
岸來
卻被太陽曬枯。

AMBITION

Create!
The soul shriek
A race with Death
Toward the goal
Whose meaning
Is created.

抱負

創造吧!
靈魂在吶喊
與死神賽跑著
奔向目標
它的意義
如斯創出。

TO THE GREGARIOUS ARTISTS
致喜好群聚的藝術家
AND JACKS-OF-ALL-TRADE
與萬事通之輩

Dam(n) that river
With all its tributaries!
Its weakened stream
Can still have some force
If you block off
The unnecessary
Channels
So that the one
Important crop
Can become fertile.

給那條支流橫生的
(該死的)河蓋座霸吧！
它日漸潺弱的主流
仍能強大起來
只要能截斷一些
無需的
支渠
這樣那唯一
重要的作物
也可因此而豐饒。

SOUTHERN HOMMAGE

to Baudelaire's "L'Albatros" and Rilke's "Der Schwann"

"Hey, Miz Albie,
"You cain't walk with them big wings;
"Don't you want me to trim 'em a little?"

"Thanks alot, Henry Willis,
"But these wings are for
"Flying,
"Or gliding."

"Ouammm, Yassum!
"But you sho' bettuh be careful
"Nobody doan'
"Step on
"One o' dem
"Befo' you takes off."

南腔致敬

致敬波特萊爾的"信天翁"與里爾克的"天鵝"

"唉哟! 阿碧小姐,
"妳不可以戴著那對大翅膀在路上亂走啦;
"讓我修剪一下它們不好嗎?"

"多謝了! 亨利威力士，
"但我得用這對翅膀
"高飛
"或低翔。"

"是哦!
"那妳最好小心點，
"別讓人
"在妳起飛前
"踩到
"任何一隻喲!"

HERZ UND DIE ZAUBERFLÖTE
Heart and the Magic Flute 心與魔笛

A camel	一隻駱駝
Set out to cross the desert	出發穿越沙漠
The sand was hot	沙很熱
She became tired	牠累了
She came upon	來到
A beautiful oasis	一個美麗的綠洲
Where she wanted to linger	牠很想稍作停留
But a voice said	卻聽到聲聲
"Keep moving forward!"	"繼續前行!"的催促
So wearily	只好疲憊的
She recommenced	再次
Her journey.	啟程。

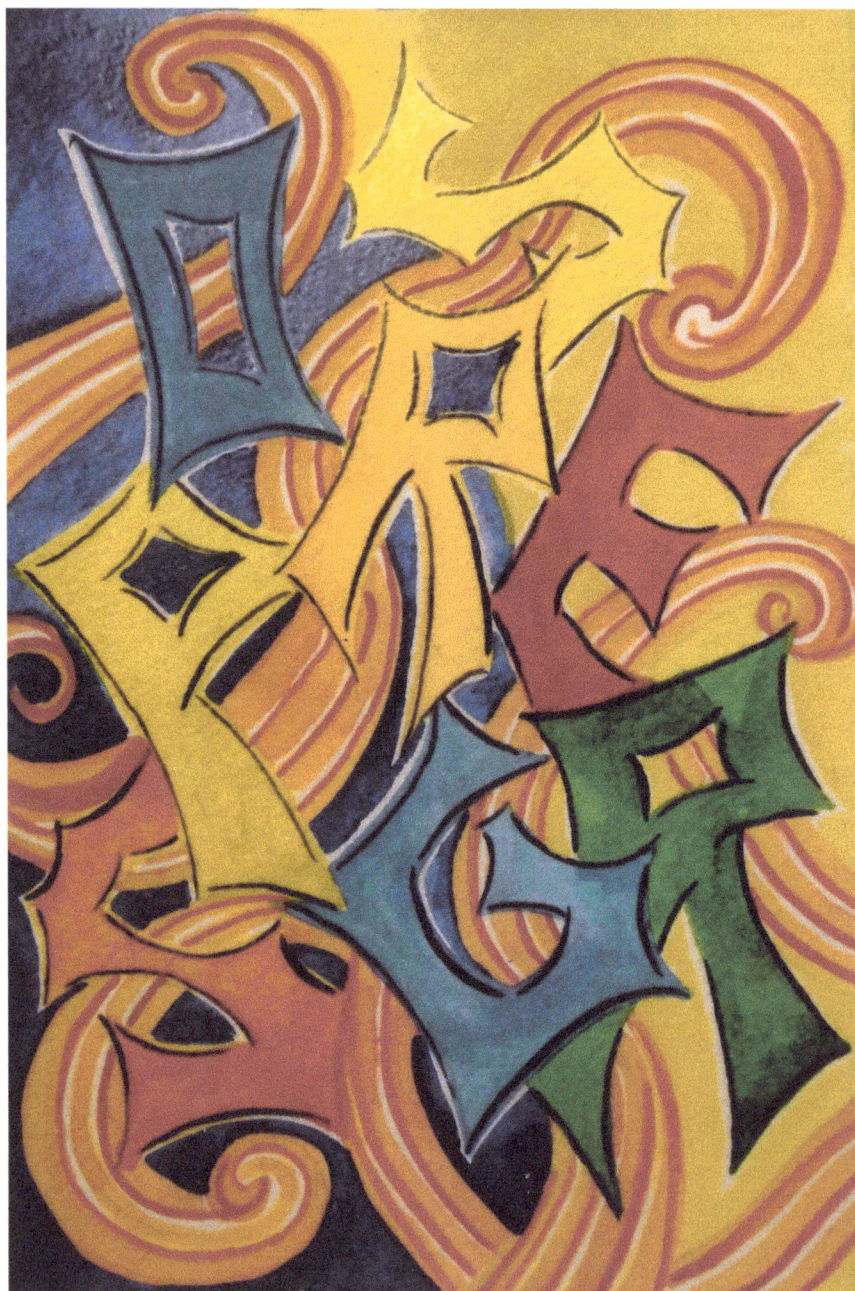

LIMERICK OF
FORWARD MOVEMENT

I think Forward Movement is nice
Learned from birds, camels, souls that entice,
    But it's easy to bog
    You can break out a cog,
Then you're stuck like a duck in the ice.

前進運動五行詩

我從心性迷人的鳥與駱駝之類
學到了勇往直前甚是可為,
    但它也易將人陷
    不容人齒輪掉鍊,
否則會如冰上困鴨進退難為。

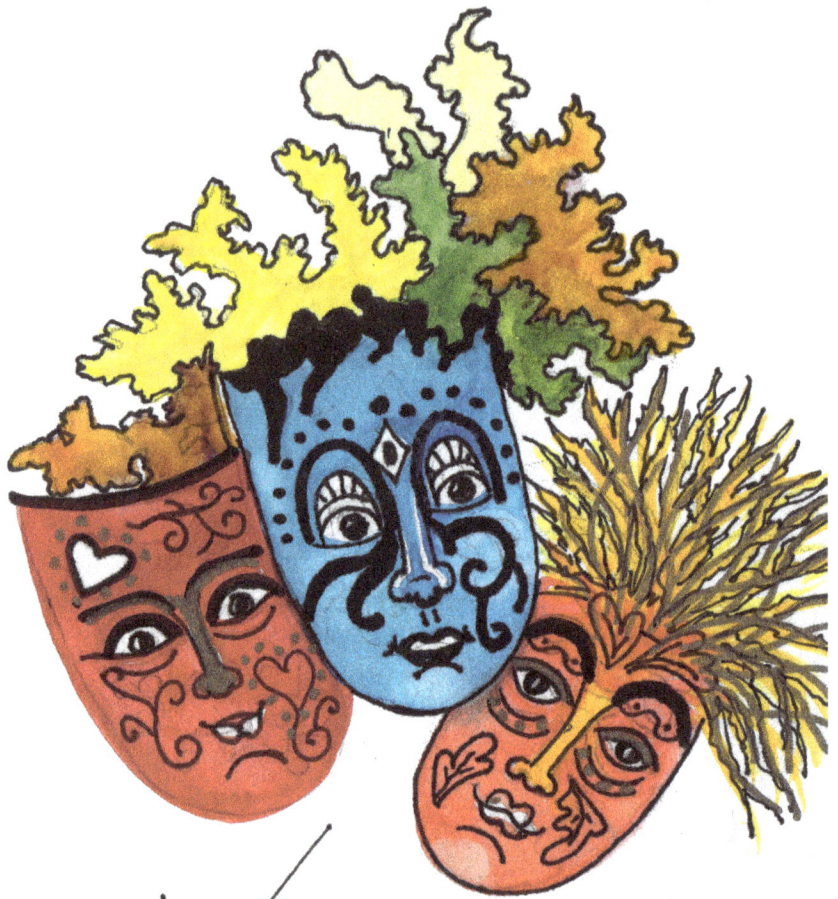

Masks
面具

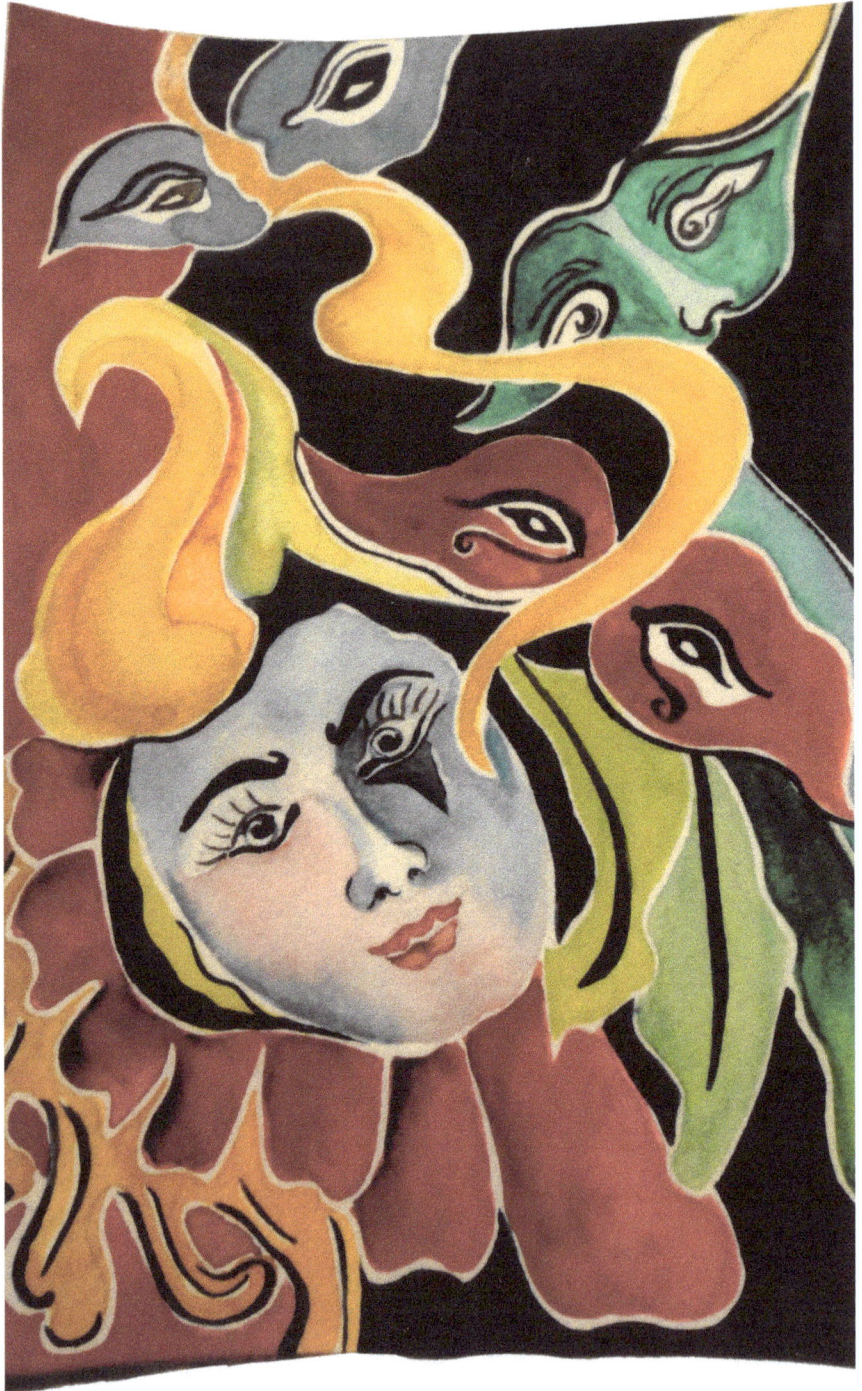

THE MASK COLLECTION
面具收藏

I went to see John,
The most popular boy in town,
And he showed me his
Mask collection.
I appreciated
His showing it to me. . . .
It meant he thought
I was
"In on" the game of life.
Now I am.

我去見過約翰，
鎮上人氣最旺的男孩，
他也讓我看了他的
面具收藏。
我很感謝
他的展示⋯⋯
這意謂著他認為
我已
"深諳"人生的遊戲。
而今我確實是。

THE MISANTHROPE

for Agnes and Margaret

My creativity is at its peak
    My mind is clicking on with rationality
But otherwise I've lost my social cheek
    It's buried in my bulk or some banality

But come and knock—I'll let you in my door
    (Don't make me go to parties and the like)
Ringing phones and some folks are a bore
    But you're a friend—you see beyond the psych

I have to put a mask on, and pretend
    To be the way I was but am no longer
My friendly self is blowing in the wind
    Perhaps it will return when I am stronger.

My fragile soul's facade is full of thorns . . .
A rose of fragrance with gargoyle horns.

厭世者

給阿格尼絲與瑪格麗特

我的創意正值巔峰
　　心中理性也響得滴答
但我的親和力已無復影蹤
　　被埋在了我的身板與庸俗之下

不過你儘可來敲門–我會讓你進來
　　(但不要叫我參加派對之類的拜託)
響不停的電話和某些人我懶得理睬
　　但你是朋友–應已將我心思揣摩

我必須戴上面具，假扮
　　那個不復存在的過去的我
和藹可親的我已隨風飄離
　　也許我夠堅強時它會再現蹤跡。

但我脆弱的心靈外表如今長滿了荊棘…
有如芬芳的玫瑰長出了怪獸之犄。

MARDI GRAS

New Orleans, 1957

Mardi Gras
Gay drunkenness
Transvestites parading in glory,
The daily mask discarded.
True selves revealed
Behind false faces;
Beneath some, happiness
Beneath others, sadness
Because Mardi Gras
Was the only day
They could be themselves.

嘉年華

新奧爾良，1957

嘉年華
同性戀者醉酒
變性者列隊展風華，
每天戴的面具已棄。
假面之後的真我
一一現形；
有人，快樂
有人，悲辛
只因唯有嘉年華
這一天
他們可以做自己。

DEPRESSION

憂鬱

An egg	一顆蛋
Looks the same from the outside	裡面空空的時候
When it is empty.	外面看起來還是一樣。
It can even be refilled	甚至可用原物質
With its substance	將它再填滿
But what happens	可是如果當它空空的時候
If outside pressure crushes it	就被外力碾了
While it is empty?	會怎樣?

COMMUNICATION

溝通

Locked	鎖在
In a glass globe	玻璃球內
Beating	敲打
Screaming	尖叫
No one hears	無人聽得見
Feign enjoyment	那偽裝的歡愉
Curious masses crush	好奇的群眾能識破否
?	?

SISYPHA LARVATA PRODEAT

Je me cache dans une langue étrangère

Je suis rentrée à Paris
dans une Triomphe TR-4
Pour recommencer mes études de flûte
avec Jean-Pierre Rampal.
La voiture de sport
était mon masque de frivolité
pendant que je travaillais beaucoup
pour rattraper le temps perdu.
À l'image d'avancer en masque
"larvata prodeat"
J'ai ajouté l'image existentialiste
de Sisyphe de Camus avec sa pierre
mais il est devenu "Sisypha"
et elle montait la colline abrupte
masquée par une triomphe.

SISYPHA WEARING A MASK ADVANCES

I hide myself in a foreign language

I returned to Paris
In a Triumph TR-4
To "Re-begin" my study of the flute
With Jean-Pierre Rampal.
The sports car
Was my mask of frivolity
While I practiced a lot
To make up for lost time.
To the image of advancing while wearing a mask,
Masked she advances
I have added the existential image
Of Camus' Sisyphus with his rock
But he has become "Sisypha"
And she climbed the steep hill
Masked by a triumph.

薛西法假面潛行
我藏身於一門外語

我開著TR-4勝利號跑車
返回巴黎
與尚–皮耶·郎帕爾老師
"重啟"長笛的學習。
為了彌補過去浪費的時光
我練得很勤
那輛跑車
則是我假裝輕佻的面具。
在女孩戴著面具往前行的
"假面潛行"形象上
我又加上了卡繆的薛西佛司與巨石
那個存在主義形象
只不過他變成了"薛西法"女孩
而她爬上了陡峭的山坡
戴著勝利的面具。

LIMERICK OF OUTWARD CONFORMITY
(masks)

for Gaddis Geeslin

Once a gal with a teflon facade
Had a politics meeting with God
   "Listen, Sis," said the Prelate,
   "If to people you'd relate,
"Wear a smile, dress in style, don't act odd."

對外看齊(面具)五行詩

給蓋第司·紀思靈

有個女孩披掛鐵氟龍外衣
與神討論政治議題
   "聽著，姑娘，"主教勸她，
   "如果想要被群眾接納，
"妳得面帶笑容，穿著合時，不標新立異。"

Politics and Arson
政治與縱火

A VISIT TO H...

See that town in the valley
Through the mist?
You are going there soon.
But don't forget to return!
A labyrinthian air
Will almost make you forget
That you want to come back
To the mountain top.
Only a tiny ray of sunlight
Through the clouds
Will make you remember.

訪H…

穿過迷霧
看到山谷中那城了嗎?
你很快就會去到那兒。
但不要忘了回來!
那迷宮似的氛圍
會令你幾乎忘了
還想回到
這山頂上來。
唯有一絲陽光
穿過雲層
才會令你再想起。

POEM FOR A ROCK SONG

The Heathen's come to town
He's gonna burn your buildings down
Is your history gonna crumble
As the bricks begin to tumble?
You were civilized 'neath the starry skies
Has decadence set in?

Oh yeah the Heathen's come to town
He's gonna kick good folks around
He hates your good manners
And your genteel traditions
If you get in his way
There will be inquisitions
The Law is complacent
It's no help to you
Your strength it is waning,
Your numbers are few
So take out your notebooks
Before memories blur
And record for posterity
The way things were.

一首搖滾詩

異教徒已然進城
他會將你們的建築燒焚
當磚塊開始滾墜
歷史會否隨之崩潰?
星空之下你本文明
腐敗是否已悄然孳生?

噢耶異教徒已然進城
他會將好人任意欺凌
他會痛恨你的彬彬有禮
和你的傳統紳士風度
如果你試圖擋他的路
會遭到嚴處
法律已自以為是
於你無助
你的力量正在萎縮,
來日已不多
不如立即掏出紙筆
趕在記憶糢糊之前
為後來者
將往事細說。

POEM IN ANGRY DESOLATION

I was only a competent working musician
And would gladly have stayed in that single position
Until they burned the building down,
And patterns of greed were easily found,
And nefarious deeds gained quiet renown
As the Wrecking Crew kept tearing things down.

I said, "What's happening to our town?
"Can somebody tell me the profit angle
"In desecrating Sam Houston's quadrangle?
"Who's getting money under the table
"To keep their wives in mink and sable?
"Who are the lobbyists on the state level?"
Their karma will send them one day to the devil.
It must be a firm of big construction
With tentacles of fiscal suction
To keep the little fish in tow
Throughout the state university row.

I will say this—it makes me sick
To see our past destroyed so quick
Because of a greedy power clique.
So now to music, I've added "sleuth"
To dig through the dirt and find the truth
And maybe our beloved "Old Main"
Won't have been destroyed in vain.

一首悲憤詩

我只不過是個稱職的音樂工作者
本可在那崗位一直愉快的待著
沒想到他們竟將那樓燒掉，
貪婪事迹清楚明瞭，
劣行卻博得暗中叫好
有如「摧毀大隊」專事惡搞。

我這才問："咱們這城怎麼了？
"誰能告訴我，如此褻瀆山姆休士頓方場，
有何利可圖？
"是誰在私下收受賄賂，
讓老婆披貂炫富？
"又是那些人遊說於州政府？"
業報指日會將他們全送至魔鬼處。
一定是有個建築公司龐大
吸金有如章魚的八爪
使得整條大學巷的小魚兒們呀
不敢不聽話。

我要說–這事我一想起就惱火
我們的往事竟然如此迅速被淹沒
只為有貪圖權勢的一小撮。
因此音樂之外我更自任"偵查"
欲將真相自灰燼中掘挖
好讓我們心愛的"老主樓"
不致白白被蹧蹋。

A CONVERSATION OVERHEARD IN A DREAM

A: Tonight's the night.

B: Why tonight?

A: In a few days it'll be much harder to burn—it's gonna be declared an archaeological landmark, and then they'll protect it—you know—smoke detectors, sprinkler systems—all that stuff.

B: But music students practice there all night—whatta' we goin' to do about that?

A: They've all gone to the big music teacher meetin' in San Antonio.

B: But the place is lit up with spotlights!

A: They're cuttin' 'em off tonight at midnight, just for us.

B: Ummm! Well ain't that sweet! You got the fire starter?

A: Yeah. Picked it up at different places in Houston.

B: Good idea. When do we get paid?

A: After the job's done. He'll meet us on Possum Walk when he sees the flames, then we hightail it south of the border.

B: But won't people know it's arson?

A: Naw! They'll just think it was faulty wiring . . . anyhow lots of guys before him wanted to tear it down.

B: Why?

A: They tell me it's been a pain in the ass—always something to fix . . . They say we must look to the future instead of the decaying past.

B: And I guess they call that "Progress."

A: Well as a matter of fact—

B: Listen! Those windows—it'll be like burning a church!

A: Don't think about it. Just think of the money. Light it up and run like hell.

B: But won't they find the cans?

A. We're gonna take them with us, stupid.

B: But what if it spills on the grass and leaves a path of flame? Won't they know?

A: Nobody will notice—they'll all be looking up. And I doubt if there will even be much of an investigation 'cause folks in Huntsville—well they just don't see Evil—they couldn't believe someone would deliberately destroy their most important landmark. Anyhow, we'll make it look like some music kid did it.

B: How?

A: Well, he said to go to the music building and vandalize some pianos and percussion—they leave that stuff out unprotected—it'll be easy.

B: Hmph! Glad he gave us a master key to the campus buildings.

A: Yeah. Might want to burn Peabody next.

B: I don't think we better push our luck—somebody might get wise.

A: Not until it's too late.

B: But wont they know someone has the key?

A: Naw—we'll open a bunch of windows—the kids do that all the time so they can get in to practice late at night—no security around here—you know that.

B: Well . . . seems O.K. to me. Guess we're in the clear. Let's go do it! Trash the instruments and burn Old Main.

夢中偶聞

A: 就在今晚了!

B: 為什麼今晚?

A: 因為過幾天會更難—它會被列為古蹟,然後受到保護,被裝上—你知道的—防火器呀,灑水系統那些個東西。

B: 可是音樂系的學生們整晚都會在那兒練習,怎麼辦?

A: 他們已經都到聖安東尼市參加音樂教師大會去了。

B: 可是那兒還是有照明燈呀。

A: 為了我們,今晚他們會將那些關掉。

B: 太好了! 有起火的傢伙嗎?

A: 有! 從休士頓各處收集來的。

B: 想得周到! 那我們何時收錢?

A: 事成之後。看到火起,他便會在頗西街與我們碰頭。然後我們得迅速往南逃過邊界。

B: 不會有人懷疑縱火嗎?

A: 不會,人們只會想到電線走火…反正之前已經有很多人想將這樓拆了。

B: 為甚麼?

A: 聽說它很傷腦筋—總是有這呀那呀的要修…他們還說應該放眼未來,不是腐朽的過去。

B: 我猜他們叫那"進步"。

A: 嗯,正是—

B: 聽著!那些窗子-說是燒了它們就像燒掉一間教堂。

A: 不要想那個了。想想錢,放把火,然後死命逃吧。

B: 不會有人發現這些罐子嗎?

A: 我們會全帶走的,笨蛋。

B: 萬一有些灑在草地上,燒出一道火痕,也看不出來嗎?

A: 不會有人注意-人們通常只會往上看。我也懷疑會有任何調查。H城的居民-眼裡沒有魔鬼-他們很難想像有人會故意摧毀這麼重要的一個城標。況且,我們會把它做得像是個音樂系的小子幹的。

B: 怎麼做?

A: 他要我們到音樂教室,故意破壞些個鋼琴或打擊樂器之類的-那些會隨便放在外頭不收起來,很容易的。

B: 嗯! 幸好他還給了我們一把校區的萬用鑰匙。

A: 是呀! 接下來把匹巴蒂樓也燒了吧。

B: 不能這麼貪心,當心有人會識破。

A: 就是識破也遲了。

B: 難道他們不會懷疑我們有鑰匙?

A: 不會-我們會故意讓一些窗子開著-那些小子們夜間練習都是如此進出-那兒沒有警衛-你知道的。

B: 嗯! 好像一切O.K.,沒障礙了。讓我們這就去搗毀樂器,將那"老主樓"燒了吧!

LIMERICK OF ARSON

Once some people of cynical turn
Chose a lovely old landmark to burn
    From all blame they escaped
    But the town had been raped
And its anger continued to churn.

縱火五行詩

曾經有些人心存不軌
將一個老城標燒燬
    他們逃過了一切懲處
    但全城的人已同遭姦汙
憤怒之情持續翻攪不退。

de l'Amour non partagé

不能分享的愛

THE AMATURE HORTICULTURIST

I went out to my garden
to plant a red rose
but its roots had already been nourished
in other soil
and it would not take root in my garden.
So I left it in its own container
And watered it lovingly.
Soon a new bud appeared,
but it was weakened
by the older flower
and by the elsewhere nurished roots.
Could I have plucked this older bloom
Even when its thorns defied my attempt?

業餘園藝家

我在自家花園
種下一株紅玫瑰
可是它已先吸收了
別家的養分
無法再在我處生根。
所以我將它留在原盆
悉心澆水照顧。
新的花苞於是很快長出，
但是先前開的花
與別處滋養的根
卻令它萎靡不振。
也許縱使前花有刺難以下手
我還是應該早早將它摘除?

POUR HELMUT VON KRIES

Apollon, beau dieu grec,
C'est tragique ta façade de glace—
insaissisable sans le savoir
aux émotions mortelles
qui ont tapé des mélodies chaleureuses
sur ta cithare,
la dernière part de ton âme à se glacer
ou est-ce la première à s'éveiller?

FOR MY GERMAN APOLLO *(translation)*

Apollo, handsome Greek god,
How tragic your icy facade—
Unwittingly elusive to human emotions
Which have played warm melodies
On your Dionysian flute,
The last part of your soul to become glacial,
Or is it the first to awaken?

給我的德國阿波羅

阿波羅，英俊的希臘神祇，
何其不幸您冰冷的面孔–
不自覺的讓人類難以情感揣摩
不知他們用您酒神的長笛
吹出的溫暖曲子，
是您最後即將冰封的心靈，
還是大夢才要初醒呢？

FISHIN' TRIP

釣魚行

Wall, ah went fishin'
Th'other day
With a piece o' lamb heart
From Safeway
For mah bait.
I cast it way far out on the lake
And it landed on an iceberg
'n just stuck to it.
Wull fin'lly the ice thawed a little bit
And ah reeled mah hook back in
"cause th' line wuz strong,
But ther' wudn't much bait left.

前天
我去釣魚
用 Safeway超市買來的
一片羊心肉
當餌。
我將它遠遠甩到湖中
但它落在一塊浮冰上
立刻就被粘住。
等冰終於化了點
我趕緊將鉤收回
因為魚線雖然夠強，
餌卻可能快沒。

A TITILLATION

I am infatuated . . .
No longer lucid but lost in a cloud.

I'm afraid to tell him
    I wonder if it shows?
With thoughts could I compel him?
    I wonder if he knows?

In dreams we come together—
    It's passionate and deep
If friendship could begin it
    There'd be something then to keep

If ever Fate stepped in a' bossing
    Like a magnet from some sphere
"Though now your paths are crossing,
    "Yours may lead you far from here."

How could he ever love me?
    I am distant and I'm shy.
And how could I be good for him?
    Oh God, I'd like to try.

And would he then be good for me—
    Encouraging my art?
And am I smart enough to see
    "The readings on the chart?"

I'm standing on the threshold
    Afraid to start, to go,
Perhaps he won't reciprocate
    Perhaps I'll never know.

動情

我已著迷…
神智不清如陷雲霓。

心事不敢告知他
　　但也許已經外露？
己意能否強加他？
　　也許他已心中有數？

夢中我們終相聚–
　　情深意也切
友情若能自此開啟
　　他日或能留得念想幾些

如天外一顆磁石飛落
　　命運之神竟也前來干預
"雖然你倆的步履在此交錯，
　　"你的卻會帶你自此遠去。"

他怎麼可能愛我？
　　我既害羞又冷漠。
我又如何能讓他有所獲？
　　老天，我很願意一搏。

那麼他也可能有助於我–
　　能鼓勵我的藝術嗎？
我的聰明才智足以讓我
　　識得"天機"嗎？

我正站在一個關口
　　不敢開步，不敢走，
他可能永不知回報
　　我也可能永遠看不透。

A CYNICAL VIEW 嘲諷之見

And so a twilight	暮色掩至
Upon a love that never was,	一段幾乎是，
But almost.	卻從來不是的愛情。
A blissful cloud of no foundation	飄浮不定的祥雲
Touching me with the illusion	拂我以
Which is happiness.	幸福的幻影。
A surging tide leaving behind it	洶湧的退潮留下
Shells, of memories, sensations	回憶與感性的貝殼
To collect.	讓人拾撿。
Two comets in irregular orbit	兩顆無定軌的彗星
Crossing by chance	偶然交會
And nevermore?	就此不再嗎?
From mine I call, "I love you,"	我從這兒喊出，"我愛你，"
Then greater the predestined distance.	命定的距離更行更遠。

SMOTHERLY LOVE

hommage to Philip Wylie

The child loved the kitten
She hugged it close
And couldn't understand
Why it quit breathing.

窒息的愛

向飛利普·威利致敬

小女孩很愛她的貓咪
將牠緊緊抱在懷裡
她只是不懂
為何牠竟停止了呼吸。

HYPERSENSITIVITY

When you extend your heart out upon a platter,
The normal thing for "civilized" cannibals
Is to prick it with a fork.
Then you have two heartaches—
One, of the effect,
The other, because you didn't know
They were cannibals,
And inadvertent members
Of the throat-cutting society—
That is, following the normal path
Of human behavior.

超級敏感

當你將心擱在餐盤上，
"文明"的食人族通常會
用叉子去戳。
你會因此感到兩種心痛－
一是由於被戳，
另一是你沒想到
他們竟是食人族，
割喉社會裡，
一群不多想的成員－
也就是說，只是依循人類行為的
正常腳步行事而已。

TO MY PINK RABBIT

Once a being of good heart
And a touch of soul poetry
Loved a youth
As middle age, the end of autumn
Crept upon him with cold fingers.
The youth followed the noble sage
Seeking the stability of age.
But she needed the vibrance of summer warmth
To mature from a bud of promise
To a flower of perfect beauty.
As her strength faded in the cold climate
She pulled away desperately
To run back to the life-giving sun,
Knowing that summer, by right, was still hers,
And that fleeting life must be tasted
In its full essence
While it was still hers for the having.

給我的粉紅兔

從前有個善良
且心存詩意的人
在哀樂中年，深秋冰冷的手指
已悄然上身之時
愛上了一個少女。
少女心儀熟齡的穩重
亦願追隨高貴的智者。
但她也需要盛夏的活力
才能自一粒充滿希望的蓓蕾
出落成一朵完美的花。
因此寒天使她日漸孱弱之時
她只好奮力掙脫
再奔赴生機盎然的太陽，
心中了然自己仍有權擁有夏天，
也明白了生命轉瞬即逝
要想充分品其精華
得把握仍擁有它時。

"DREAM"

final song from Platristogynes,
a comédie-ballet dedicated to Karen Carter

Dream, dream,
Touch the daydream
The air's burning
Your heart's yearning
To find your lover and to hold him
Very close . . .
Forever!

Dream, dream,
Touch the daydream
Your loves are pure
And long may they
Endure through this life
And into all of the others,
Believe me!

This love that you have
Can be a friendship, admiration
Or a passion.
Every person on the earth
Should have the right to love
In his own fashion.

And I will say it once more . . .
He whom you adore
Let your passions soar
Bring them to the fore
Ending never more
You dreamers,
Awake
To your dream
Come true!

"夢"

Platristogynes芭雷喜劇的
最後一曲,獻給凱倫·卡特

夢,夢,
做個白日夢
空氣在燃燒
你的心也正熱烈渴望
找到你的愛人並將他
永遠的…
抱緊!

夢,夢,
做個白日夢
你的愛很純淨
它們會貫穿
此生
以及所有的來世,
請相信!

你擁有的愛
可以是友情,慕情
或激情。
世上每個人
都應該有權
以自己的方式動情。

我要再說一遍…
對你所戀
要激情飛躍
要放在眼前
要永不止歇
做夢的人兒啊,
美夢
成真
再醒覺!

ORPHEUS

a lute song for Robert Veyron-Lacroix

Orpheus wandered into the shades
In search of the memory of a song
And found a lost soul who there had strayed
And led her back the pathway long.

Orpheus looked Death straight in the face,
So handsome and kind, with strength all to bear,
Courageously choosing Perfection's Race,
Knowing it hopeless, but without a care.

Orpheus dares not believe that she,
While searching the only worthwhile thing,
Has seen these things as clearly as he,
Chosen happiness in his life to bring.

To worship and love him from far or near,
And play him the music of the spheres.

奧菲斯

長笛曲贈羅伯·威宏－克拉羅

奧菲斯漫步至陰暗之地
為尋記憶中之一曲
發現有個迷失的靈魂也流落那裏
帶她走長長的甬道回去。

奧菲斯與死神直面相對，
英俊善良無比，且使盡全力，
勇敢與祂比賽完美，
明知無望，但不介意。

可是奧菲斯不敢相信，
她致力尋思生命何事最值，
已如他般將世事看盡，
竟選擇為他帶來一生樂事。

愛他崇他不辭遠近，
只想為他奏出天籟之音。

LOVE AND PIG LIMERICK

Tho' love's like a prize to be won,
And admittedly sometimes is fun,
    Like a tasty repast
    For a pig doesn't last,
Love can fade with the light of the sun.

愛情與豬五行詩

雖說愛情有如獎品可以贏得，
說實話有時還滿有得樂，
    但就似豬食可口
    留不久，
愛情也會在陽光下褪色。

Friends

友儕

A JAZZ SONNET IN 5/4

for Maggie Foster, Dewitte and Sterling Lindsey

Today the Muse did visit me again
    Your friendship's inspiration means so much
More notes for "Maggie's Waltz" sprang from my pen
    And from piano keys that I did touch

Your spirit free does wander where it will
    Mirage the camel sees upon the sand
And strength and creativity do fill
    My thoughts because I know you'll understand

But if tomorrow you should go away
    As beauteous spirits often seem to do
The gift you've given me, I know, will stay
    Creating beauty as I think of you.

It's like a ring of gold that has no end—
The thanks I joyfully give to you, my friend.

5/4拍的爵士樂十四行詩

給瑪姬·福斯特，德威特和司德靈·林賽

今日繆思女神再度光顧
　　你的友情令我靈感四出
得以為"瑪姬的華爾滋"這齣
　　自筆下琴上譜出更多音符

你的自由意志奔放不羈
　　有如駱駝在沙漠中看到的幻影
我的思緒充滿了力量與創意
　　只因知道有你的肯定

也許明天你就會離開
　　美好的精靈總是不久待
但你賜我的禮物卻會常在
　　想妳時美好創意會源源流出來。

朋友! 一環金戒無始終–
我對你的感激也不知盡頭。

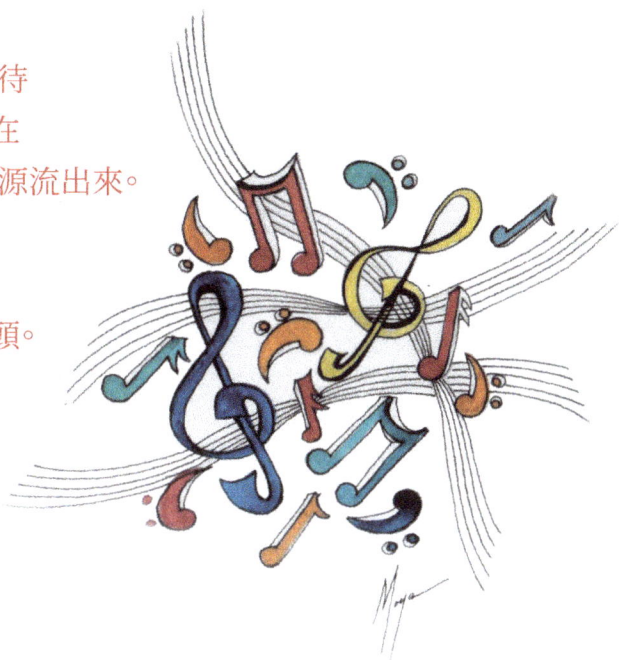

DUO FOR MEZZO AND FLUTE
女中音與長笛協奏

to Beverly Evans
給比佛利·伊凡司

Moonlight	月光
Lucid	清澈
But not	不若
Sun-blinding	陽光刺目
Gentle and cool	溫柔又清涼
Belle et profonde.	美好且雋永。

POUR ROBERT VEYRON-LACROIX

Ta nonchalence détachée des masses,
ton art qui est resplendissant,
ton masque de légèreté
qui protege ta sensibilité,
O, être charmant et profond,
dont les yeux reflètent la tristesse,
tu a réussi à me désarmer,
moi, qui porte aussi déguisement,
Et donc, ton amie, si tu as jamais besoin,
je suis, pour toute l'éternité.

FOR ROBERT VEYRON-LACROIX
(a translation)

Your nonchalant detachment from the mass
    Your artistry which shines so brilliantly
The mask of légèreté which you possess
    Which but protects your sensitivity

Your personal depth, enchanting in its charm
    which emmenates life's sadness through your eyes
Has, for all times, succeeded to disarm
    This writer, who too, often wears disguise

And so your friend if ever need there be
I am, from here unto eternity.

致羅伯·威宏-拉克羅

你與眾疏脫
    你才藝耀眼
你用冷漠
    將感性遮掩

你的深度令人著迷驚訝
    雙眼道盡人生辛酸迷茫
這一切總能輕易卸下
    我這作者也擅偽裝的心防

只要你有需要朋友之時
從今日到永遠，我都會是。

POEM FOR A BRILLIANT FRIEND
詩致一絕妙好友

Gloria Wheeler	葛洛麗·惠勒
Mindfuck joy	令我心迷神亂
Play with ideas like a toy	創意當玩具玩
Fly down lofty paths together	一起自高處飛下去
Happiness makes thought a feather	快樂思緒如羽
Khaki outfits, boots of leather	卡其裝，皮革履
Thoughts fly high without a tether	意念高飛無拘
Platonic sensuosity	柏拉圖式的情誼
Yes, your friend I'd like to be.	是的，當你的朋友我願意。

LA CONNAISSANCE DES GENS ET LA SUITE

See there the City of Iys,
Glistening beneath the surface of the water
On a sunny morn.
No, don't reach down to touch
The cathedral spires. . . .
Proximity will only blur
The distant clarity.

Shimmering and full of waves
Is now the water.

人的認知及其他

一個陽光燦爛的早晨，
看憶艾斯城
在水面下閃爍晶瑩。
不，不要彎身去碰
那主教教堂的尖頂⋯⋯
近了只會模糊
遠觀的清晰。

而今日水上
正波光搖曳。

EYES—A TRIBUTE TO DADDY

Eyes that have known death and felt pain
Eyes that show a profound love of humanity
    As the practice of your profession shows
Eyes that reflect the truest nobility—
    That of the soul
Eyes that express uncommunicable thoughts
    Of love and respect,
    Of sadness
    Of the beauty of nature
    Of humility before the immensity
      of the universe
    Of strength and courage to work
      When no energy is left—
Eyes that show a sensitivity so deep
    It is sometimes covered
      with little grassburrs
      that are felt when one touches
      a tender spot in talk.
As I grow older and sometimes think deep thoughts
    I see a kinship of your eyes with my own.

眼睛—獻給父親

那雙眼見過死亡感過痛楚
那雙眼因職業使然
　　　流露對人性最深的關懷
那雙眼反映了來自靈魂的-
　　　真正高貴
那雙眼傳達了難以言喻的
　　　愛與尊重
　　　哀傷
　　　對大自然的欣賞
　　　面對宇宙浩瀚的
　　　　　謙卑
　　　以及力盡了仍工作不息的-
　　　　　堅強與勇氣
那雙眼感性如此之深
　　　言到椎心處
　　　　　有時會讓人感到
　　　　　那兒長滿了
　　　　　帶刺的小草
在我年事漸長思慮漸深之際
　　　看到那雙眼有如看到自己。

TWO DON QUIJOTES 兩位唐吉軻德

to Bob Oliveira   *給鮑伯·奧利維亞*

Two don Quijotes	兩位唐吉軻德
Jousting	太理想主義的
Idealistically	在為不可能之事
The impossible	比武對決
But wait!	且慢!
Can't Will	就不能讓
Have more force	叫意志的
Than	強過
Fate?	叫命運的嗎?

A NOTE IS PLAYED

for Dorothy Dow

A note is played,
and after the vibrations die
I can hear the note clearly,
or I look at the sun through smoked glass,
or I jump on the merry-go-round running.
But you
are music with ever-elusive sound,
brilliant light that smoked glass
can't fathom . . .
Your orbit I can only vaguely follow
in parallel motion.

一聲音符奏出

給桃樂絲·道

一聲音符奏出,
它的振動消逝之後
我仍能聽得清楚,
就像我可以透過暗色玻璃直視太陽,
或跳上正在行進中的旋轉木馬。
而你
卻是教人永遠抓不住樂音的曲子
一道暗色玻璃也無法透視的
強光⋯
你運轉的軌道我只能勉強的
平行追隨。

SONNET IN "SHANGHAI EAST"

for Rudy Jenkins

It's such a fragile thread we're hanging by
    As you and I traverse the sea of life
With changing masks of friends and passersby
    (Caused by balances of love and strife)

Lethal pressures nail us to the wall
    But Cupid's arrows counteract our plight
Is Love but an opium after all,
    Whose fair illusions blind us for the night?

And what's the place of Art in all of this?
    How can you separate it from the rest?
Life is an Art and Art is loving bliss
    Of all the three, Art is the perfect quest:

While Life has limits and Love fades away,
Our Art lives on forever and a day.

"浦東"裏的十四行詩

給魯迪詹金斯·堅肯士

我倆航行在人生之海
　　關係危如游絲搖擺
朋友與路人的面具輪流著戴
　　(能平衡只因有爭執也有愛)

致命的壓力將我們釘死在牆
　　邱比特的箭卻為我們解壓
難道愛情只能將鴉片充當
　　美好幻覺讓我們一夜眼瞎?

這其中藝術又佔了何位?
　　你又如何將它與他事區別?
人生是一門藝術,藝術令人陶醉
　　三者之中,藝術最可追:

生命有其限,愛情會消褪,
惟有藝術長命百歲。

POUR JEAN-PIERRE RAMPAL

J'hésitais au commencement
du chemin de la perfection
quand je t'ai vu
de très loin, vers le sommet.
D'une manière magique
Tu m'as montré la bonne route.
Maintenant, toujours en train
mais quand même un peu plus loin
je te vois encore là-haut.
Et avec plus de compréhension
je t'admire autant que jamais,
Monsieur Rampal,
Ma personnification de la perfection.

FOR MONSIEUR RAMPAL
致郎帕爾大師
a free translation

Just pausing at the beginning　　駐足在完美之途的
Of perfection's path　　起始點
I first saw you　　我初次見到
Far ahead in the distance.　　您在前方離我甚遠。
With magical insight　　您以神奇的見識
You showed me the way　　為我領路
And inspired me to persevere.　　並鼓勵我要堅持。
Now, farther along the path　　而今走過大段路
Where the light shines brighter　　四下已越見光明
I see you still ahead　　您仍在前
But with deeper understanding　　但我已更能深識
And appreciation　　與體會
Of your greatness.　　您的宏偉。

"AKASHA"

Furryburrytawnycat

Lounging

By the pool in a chair

With the wind in your hair

And a contemplative air

On top of the world just waiting

Thinking, planning, and creating

Tired of New York rat races

So Manhattanmice come to you instead

To be put through their paces . . .

(And a West Coast Rodent waiting in the wings)

"阿卡夏"

一隻毛髮蓬鬆棕色貓

懶洋洋的趴在

池畔的椅子上

風從髮間吹過

您以沉思之姿

在世界之巔就這麼等著

想著，計畫著，創造著

終於有一群曼哈頓之鼠

厭倦了紐約的瘋狂鼠賽

選擇到您這兒來重整腳步…

(還有一隻西海岸碩鼠在一旁等待)

A DACTYLIC MEANDERING

I like to reflect on this life as I see it
And once in a while I descend to the fray
    To write a new musical,
    Play on an instrument,
Juggle ennui in a profitable way.

But thanks to an Angel some people appear
Changing the course of my life's crablike gait
    Tho' slobby, I clean up
    My place and buy flowers
And put engineering and math on my plate.

With new motivation, I fly to the stars . . .
"Come hear my new music and read my new play
    "Please show me your sketches
    "And poems and sculptures
"And let's talk of Beckett, Proust, Dante, Genet.

Talk of duration of friendship, the senses,
Please come in my mind and we'll go for a ride
    Jealousy tries
    To attack our defenses
But Friendship's a castle, the moat, it is wide.

婉約長短調

我喜歡反映此生所見
每隔一陣就會墮入瞎忙當中
　　或寫齣新音樂劇,
　　或玩個新樂器,
化無聊為有利可圖。

然而感謝天使讓某些人出現
將我生活中的無狀改變
　　我清除了髒亂
　　在居處插上花
還將工程與數學咀嚼。

帶著新動力,我興致高飛…
"請來聽聽我的新曲,讀讀我的新劇
　　"也讓我看看你們的素描
　　"你們的詩與雕塑
"讓我們來聊聊貝克特,普魯斯特,但丁和吉內特。"

聊聊友誼與理性能維持多長,
請進入我的內心,將一個遊戲玩
　　嫉妒總想
　　攻擊我們的心防
但友誼是座城堡,它的護城河,很寬。

A PAEAN
FOR ALOIS HESSLING

I love the hours I have spent with you
    Conversing on all subjects with a grin
You are a perfect "Swann" from out of Proust
    Describing San Francisco from within.

Your gourmet taste as chef and decorator
    Could overwhelm me but I'm not surprised . . .
I saw the signs of elegant creator
    When first at "Woyzeck" I looked in your eyes

And wandered through the lighthouse of your soul
    And saw the depth of treasures scattered there
And saw good karma glowing like a coal
    And felt both kindness, humor everywhere.

And in a light with beatific flame
    Back in a corner hidden from the rest
I saw that trait that sometimes has no name
    Purefied by suff'ring—it's the best

I hope to see you many times again
Our friendship will remain through thick and thin.

一首歡樂歌
給阿洛意司·黑思靈的

我喜歡與你共度的時光
　　天南地北帶笑談
你是來自普魯斯特書裡最完美的先生"斯望"
　　將三藩市裏外描繪完。

你那大廚與室內設計師的品味
　　令我折服但不驚訝…
初次在"Woyzeck"劇裡與你會面
　　已看到一個創作者的優雅。

漫步穿過你心靈的燈塔
　　看到四處堆積著寶藏
善舉如炭火發光
　　仁慈與幽默恆常

從隱藏在一角之
　　一束聖潔光
更看到了你難以命名的特質
　　苦難淬煉過的–果然最棒

我希望能與你再多相見
願我們的友誼好壞不辭永遠。

SONNET

Explore each status quo and then decide
    While walking down Columbus, Polk or Green
If by conventions social to abide
    Or with a laugh, just flush in a latrine

The roving wolf tears off her sweet sheep's mask
    The penance of the past has turned to pleasure
On a windy hill perhaps to bask
    While culling from her mind a music treasure

A tricky Fate deals moods both low and high
    But discipline allows some recompense
New friendships start with folks of earth and sky
    And friends from other climes send love and sense

So what the future holds no one can tell
But like a spring the options start to well.

十四行詩

沿著哥倫布，波克或格林街走
　　檢視當下再行動
看是世俗規範守
　　抑或一笑沖馬桶

惡狼撕了羊假面
　　往日苦修轉貪戀
嶺上讓山風撲臉
　　心中將音樂揀選

造化不辨心高低
　　自律才能獲回應
友情起始無貴賤
　　他鄉亦傳愛與情

未來難料不好言
選擇卻會如湧泉。

THE EAGLET

for Lois Cole

Don't push the young eagle
Out of his nest
Before maturity gives him
Strong claws and wings
Covered by impregnable feathers.
Otherwise the lesser animals
From the jungle of humanity
Will try to kill him
Before he becomes king.

雛鷹

給露意絲·柯爾

別逼雛鷹
離巢
在牠尚未成熟
腳爪未鋒羽翼也未
堅不可摧之際。
否則人類叢林裡的
次等動物
會讓牠死在
成王之前。

CHEVALIER DE MEDICI

for Barton Brown

In the Middle Ages
The days of chivalry,
Knights had life all figured out—
They wore armor for protection . . .
The trick was to hide the sensitive areas.
Now it's the twentieth century
But once in a while
One can still find
A knight in shining armor.

麥地奇家的騎士

給巴頓·布朗

在講究騎士精神的
中世紀，
騎士們已將人生想得清晰–
他們盔甲防身…
訣竅就在將罩門藏起。
而今二十世紀
偶爾
仍能見到
一個騎士全身盔甲亮麗。

THE FEATHER CRUTCH

Have another scotch!
It will give you courage
To come down to earth
And make beautiful music.
Dumbo with the feather in your trunk
Don't you know you don't have to be drunk
To do wonderful things?
You have big ears to fly with—
We need you
We earthlings appreciate
Your great talent
We love you
We know you.

羽毛拐杖

再來一杯威士忌吧!
它會讓你有勇氣
下凡來
譜出美麗的樂曲。
長鼻上插著羽毛的小飛象啊
難道你不知道你無需喝醉
也能做出神奇的事嗎?
你有一對大耳朵可以飛呀−
我們需要你
我們這些世人能欣賞
你的天賦大才
我們愛你
我們懂你。

DIFFERENT EMPHASIS

You criticize her
Because she's a "lazy artist"
And doesn't always keep
A clean house for company.
But you know, yourself,
That if one of your patients
Was dying in the morning
You wouldn't stop
To make up the bed.

重點不同

你總批評她
說她是個"懶藝術家"
不懂待客
不會持家。
但你自己也知道，
如果你的一個病人
一早就要死了
你絕不會停下來
先把床給鋪了。

LIMERICK OF FRIENDSHIP

Although Love flows away on salt tears
A good Friendship can linger for years.
　　　But the difference between
　　　Can hardly be seen . . .
If you can, just combine them, my dears!

友情五行詩

雖說愛情總隨著鹹鹹的淚水流逝
美好的友情卻能多年維持。
　　　但兩者的區別
　　　很難察覺⋯
可以的話，親愛的，合併它倆最合適！

Afterword

When my wife and I moved to Huntsville, Texas, in 1972, we soon heard about the most remarkable siblings in this city of some 30,000: they were Tommy Cole, a physician who quietly mumbled quotations from Shakespeare, Goethe and Hardy, wrote notes in German and sang German songs, and still made house calls for his senior patients, and his sister Jan Cole who was fluent in French, having studied at the Sorbonne, and was universally acknowledged as the finest all-around musician in the geographical area—a woman who could play the piano, pipe organ, harpsichord, anything with strings ("She can pluck melody out of a tennis racquet") but whose special instrument was the flute. And for years we knew who the Coles were and why they were locally famous, but we did not know them personally.

Eventually, we did get to know them both, but Jan, I got to know and like because I once asked if she could play some Renaissance music for my little Shakespeare's birthday party for the English Department at Sam Houston State University where I taught. The celebration, we called it "Shakespeare Un-plugged," was intended for my advanced class of Shakespeare Studies—about 25 students—and anyone else who might drop in. I ordered cookies, punch, and coffee for about forty people—ten more than I expected to attend based on previous celebrations. That's when I learned just how wide-spread were Jan's friends and just how influential was her teaching. Our auditorium seats 160, but on this week-day afternoon, I found myself scrambling for more chairs. We came up with twenty more, but we still didn't have enough seats. I had expected a quiet little session with soft music and some readings from the Bard. What I got was Professor Harold Hill hitting town.

Jan had arranged performances by singers and musicians—some colleagues, some former and current students, some musical friends anxious to be in on a Jan Cole afternoon. I quickly decided that my best role was to introduce the artists, read a few appropriate passages from the Bard and get out of the way. We had over 180 people that afternoon, many from cities two hundred or more miles away, and at least three couples came from out of state. We had never had such a crowd before and we certainly have not had such a crowd since. That is when I learned of Jan Cole's popularity and influence.

So, for over a decade now, my wife and I have enjoyed knowing Jan Cole and listening to her play her multitude of instruments. She served as our church organist for years, and it is always a joy visiting her in her instrument-filled home. We smile watching her drive around town in her enormous Dodge pick-up, and we simply enjoy knowing this soft-spoken, friendly woman.

Then we had the honor of reading this book of Jan's poems, and learning a little of her back-story. In these poems we see the young American woman studying in Paris, scooting around Europe in her racing-green Triumph TR4

(Jan is a woman of taste). We see her enthusiasm for her musical training and her French lessons, her early sympathy and sensitivity for those who were "different," and we hear her thoughts on love and affection. She is a young woman finding herself in the world, and later as a more mature woman, she comments on what she has found through the years both inside and outside herself.

These poems have given me greater insight into this remarkably talented woman whose low, soft voice and extreme modesty belie an active and passionate inner voice—one which can express universal truths while telling her personal story. Jan's brother, Dr. Tommy Cole is a great, sympathetic doctor and one of the two or three true intellectuals in this University city; Jan Cole, we learn from these poems, is one of the others.

—Ralph Pease
2018

Ralph Pease is a native Texan who grew up in Dallas, graduated from the University of Texas, holds a PhD. from Texas A&M, served as an officer in the US Marine Corp, taught English in colleges for 44 years, and received awards and recognitions including the Minnie Stevens Piper award and induction into the College of Humanities Wall of Honor at Sam Houston State University in 2018.

後語

　　1972 年，我和妻子搬到德州的亨次維爾不久，就聽說了在這個三萬人的小城裡，住有一對不同凡響的兄妹：哥哥湯姆·柯爾是位可以娓娓誦出莎士比亞，哥德，和哈地名句，可以用德文書寫，可以唱德文歌曲，還可以為年長病人出診的醫生；妹妹珍·柯爾則是位法語流利，曾經留學法國巴黎大學，且為本地區一致公認的，最棒的全方位音樂家—一個能彈鋼琴，管風琴，大鍵琴，以及任何帶弦樂器（"她從網球拍也能摳出曲子"）的女士，不過她的特長是長笛。　多年來我們只知道有這麼倆位柯爾家的人，也知道他們為什麼有名，但並無緣親識。

　　不過我們與他們二位最終還是有緣相識了。　我之所以能結識並且很喜歡珍·柯爾，源於有一次，我為任教的山姆休士頓州立大學英語系舉辦莎士比亞慶生會，我問她可否願意來為我們演奏一些文藝復興時期的音樂。我們稱那次的慶生會為「起動莎士比亞」，一個針對我指導的「莎士比亞進階班」—大約二十五位學生—以及任何可能臨時加入的人所舉辦的活動。我事先訂了四十人份的餅乾，飲料和咖啡—根據以往的經驗，已經比預期的出席人數，多訂了十人份。　就是在那次活動，我領教了珍的交遊有多廣，以及她的教學影響有多大。　我們那個表演廳可以容納一百六十人，可是在那個不是周末的下午，我卻發現自己一直在張羅椅子。　我另外找到了二十張椅子，卻發現仍然不夠坐。　我心中設想的是一個安靜的，有輕柔音樂，有莎翁朗誦的小型活動，結果看到的卻是音樂劇裡的哈洛·修爾教授進城了。

　　珍為我們安排了歌唱與樂器的表演，表演者中有些是她的同事，有些是她過去與目前的學生，還有些是只想與珍·柯爾同在一下午的音樂界友人。　我很快就決定了自己最該扮演的角色：介紹藝術家，讀幾段適當的莎士比亞，然後迅速閃人。那個下午，出席者超過了一百八十人，其中有許多來自兩百英哩或更遠之外，至少有三對夫妻來自外州。　在那之前我們從未有過如此盛況，之後確實也未曾再有。　那一刻，我是真領教了珍·柯爾的人氣與影響力。

至今，我和妻子已經認識珍，且有幸聆聽她演奏多種樂器十多年了。她在我們的教會司琴多年，每次拜訪她那佈滿樂器的家，我們總是滿心歡喜；看到她駕著那輛巨無霸道奇卡車滿城遊走，我們也會滿臉笑意。我們真的很高興能夠認識這位親切又輕聲細語的女士。

然後，我們更覺榮幸，得以讀到她的這本詩集，因而得知了她的一些往事。在這些詩裡，我們看到一個留學巴黎的年輕美國女孩，駕著英國賽車綠的TR4勝利號跑車，馳騁歐陸(珍是個有品味的女士)；看到她學習法語與音樂很熱情；發現她早就對與眾「不同」的人士敏感且同情；也聽到她對感情與愛情有所思考。早年，她是個在全世界尋找自己的年輕女孩；後來，變成一個成熟的女人了，她就給多年來自己發現的，身內與身外的諸事下判語。

這些詩也助我更深入的領會到，這個有著非凡天賦的女人，其實在她輕柔，低沉，且極端謙虛的言語之下，還有一道激情活躍的聲響─在敘述自身故事的同時，還能表達普世真理的一道聲音。在這個大學城裏，有兩位，或三位，真正的有識之士。珍的哥哥，偉大又有情的湯姆·柯爾醫生，是其中的一位。而從這些詩看來，珍·柯爾，應該是另一位。

洛夫·皮士
2018

洛夫·皮士先生是道地的德州人，從小在達拉斯長大。他畢業自德州大學，擁有德州A&M大學的博士學位。他曾是美國海軍陸戰隊的一名軍官，至今在各大院校教授英文已達四十四年。他獲得的榮譽與認可當中包括曾獲米妮·史蒂文斯—派帕獎，以及2018年榮登山姆休士頓州大人文學院榮譽榜。

Jan Cole with Adelina Moya, Huntsville, Texas, 2018.

Biographies 簡介

Illustrator: Adelina Moya

Mexican born artist, Adelina Moya studied graphic design at the Universidad de Las Americas in Puebla, Pue., Mexico. She studied watercolor with Lopez Oliver in Monterrey, Mexico, and she studied various styles of painting at the Universidad de Monterrey. Since then, Moya has continued her artistic studies continually incorporating new styles and media. Moya's art has been shown in Puebla, Pue, Mexico, Atlixco, Pue, Mexico, Mexico City, and at numerous galleries in Texas.

作畫人：雅德琳娜·摩亞

雅德琳娜·摩亞是生於墨西哥的藝術家。她先在墨西哥普埃布拉的美利堅大學攻平面設計，後從蒙特瑞的羅培·奧利佛先生學水彩，並於蒙特瑞大學習得多種畫風。此後摩亞女士一直致力於將各種新風格與媒體共冶一爐。她的作品曾散見墨西哥的普埃布拉與亞特利斯柯，以及墨西哥市等地，也曾在德州的多家畫廊展出。

Design: Kim Davis

Kim Davis has an MFA in Creative Writing, Editing, and Publishing from Sam Houston State University in Huntsville, Texas and a BA in Arts and Entertainment Media Management from Columbia College in Chicago, Illinois.

設計：金·戴維斯

金·戴維斯女士曾於伊利諾州芝加哥市的哥倫比亞大學學習，擁有該校藝術與娛樂媒體管理的學士學位。後來她在德州亨次維爾市的山姆休士頓州立大學攻讀創作，編輯，和出版，並獲得了該校的藝術碩士學位。

Chinese Translator: Angela Liu

Angela Liu obtained a BA in Foreign Languages and Literature from the National Taiwan University in 1972. She later got an MA in English Education from the University of Kansas, in Lawrence, Kansas, and a CAGS (Certificate of Advanced Graduate Study) in Educational Media and Technology from Boston University, Boston, Massachusetts in 1974 and 1978 separately.

After a short stint of teaching English as a second language in California and Boston, she switched career to a scientific field, and took literature and writing only as a hobby. In 2014, she retired and moved back to Taiwan with her husband. The following year, she was unexpectedly connected with Lorrie Lo in Texas through a common friend, thus had a chance to try translating English poems to Chinese for the first time.

翻譯：楊愛蘭

楊愛蘭女士1972年畢業於台灣國立台灣大學外文系，隨後留學至美國堪薩斯與麻塞諸塞州，分別於1974 和1978 年獲得勞倫斯城堪州大學的英文教育碩士學位，以及波士頓大學教育媒體暨科技碩士後進修結業證。

在加州與波士頓短暫教過幾年英語為第二語之後，她轉換跑道從事科研工作，文學與寫作退居為愛好。2014年與先生一起退休回到台灣，次年通過一個共同朋友的聯繫，與住在德州的駱珞意外結緣，於是有了此次初嚐英詩中譯的機會。

Editor: Lorrie Lo Wagamon

Lorrie Lo graduated from the National Cheng Chi University in Taiwan with a BA in journalism. She and husband Dr. Charles H. Wagamon, Jr. were dedicated to broadening English horizons in Taiwan for years. She edited various magazines and published several English learning books. She even established a service agency, Nova International Cultural & Educational Services (NICES) to promote cultural exchanges.

Lorrie's special passion, however, is publishing multi-lingual poetry books. She once helped Patricia Hu, a renowned professor of French literature and a poet in Taiwan, to publish her poetry books, *The Falling Flowers* and *Tang Poems of Ancient Melodies* in Chinese, English, and French. Those two books made great impressions on Jan Cole, a popular and well respected musician and poet of Huntsville,

Texas, where Lorrie lived since 2014. Lorrie and Jan met and became dear friends. Jan wished to see her English and French poems also shown in Chinese, and Lorrie promised to make her dream come true. The path toward that dream has not been without obstacles, but Lorrie has been lucky to be in contact with a volunteer translator thousands of miles away, and with whose help she was, in the end, able to keep her promise and happily see the tri-lingual *Sisypha Larvata Prodeat* on its way.

編譯：駱珞
駱珞女士1972 年畢業自台灣國立政治大學新聞系。她和先生魏徹德博士曾在台灣推廣英語多年。她也曾主編多種雜誌，出版過數本英語讀本，並成立了洛華國際文教中心鼓吹文化交流。

但他最熱衷的卻是出版多語詩集。她曾幫助台灣的法國文學教授，也是名詩人的胡品清女士出版中英法三語詩集「落花」與「唐詩古韻」。那兩本詩集在駱珞於2014 年搬至美國德州亨次維爾長居時，給當地的知名音樂家暨詩人珍·柯爾女士留下了深刻的印象。兩人成為至友後，珍表示也想看到自己的英法文詩能以中文出現，駱珞立刻就答應幫她圓夢。實現那個夢想的道路並不平坦，但駱珞意外得到了千里之外一位譯者的鼎力相助，最後終於能信守承諾，並欣然看到三語詩集「薛西法假面潛行」的到來。

Acknowledgments

With deep appreciation to Dr. Chueh Chang, Dr. Yi-Fei Chen, Dr. and Mrs. Charles Wagamon, Dr. and Mrs. Ralph Pease, Barbara Sloan, Marcus Jones, Diffoung Chang, Kay Chu, Terri Jones, Jian Zheng, Cathy Teng, Kang Xuepei, Jen Sun, Elaine Chen, Wei-Na Lee, Sue Hwei Hsieh, Chia Wei Fu and Sylvia Jahn for their consultation on translation and proofreading of English, French, and Chinese.

致謝

此詩集成書期間，承蒙張珏博士，陳一飛博士，查理士·魏格曼博士夫婦，洛夫·皮士博士夫婦，芭芭拉·史隆，馬可仕·鍾斯，張蝶風，朱道凱，魏台麗，鄭建青，Cathy Teng，康雪培，孫人先，陳雅玲，李威娜，曾夙慧，姚嘉為，于錫娜等諸親友不吝撥冗賜教，於中英法三語給予意見，參予校正，不勝感激之至。

www.ingramcontent.com/pod-product-compliance
Lightning Source LLC
Chambersburg PA
CBHW050823090426
42738CB00020B/3462